THE EUCHARIST

A Mystery of Faith

Joseph M. Champlin

Paulist Press
New York/Mahwah, N.J.

Imprimatur:
+Most Reverend Thomas J. Costello, DD
Vicar General, Diocese of Syracuse, New York
Feast of St. Mark the Evangelist, April 25, 2005

Cover design by Cindy Dunne

Library of Congress Cataloging-in-Publication Data

Champlin, Joseph M.
    The Eucharist : a mystery of faith / Joseph M. Champlin.
        p. cm.–(IlluminationBook)
    ISBN 0-8091-4363-1 (alk. paper)
    1. Lord's Supper–Catholic Church. 2. Mass. 3. Catholic Church–Doctrines.
I. Title. II. IlluminationBooks.
    BX2215.3.C48 2005
    234'.163–dc22

                                                                    2005011940

Published by Paulist Press
997 Macarthur Boulevard
Mahwah, New Jersey, 07430

www.paulistpress.com

Printed and bound in the United States of America

Contents

Introduction

When I was finding my way back to God, I started attending daily and weekend Masses at the Cathedral. During every Mass I attended, I would begin to cry when we said, "I am not worthy to receive, but only say the word and I shall be healed." The most important part of the Mass to me was receiving the Eucharist, but I was not worthy. After I was confirmed, I continued to cherish the Eucharist, but never thought I would be worthy to serve as a Eucharistic Minister. When Father Champlin asked me if I would be a Eucharistic Minister at weekend Mass, I told him that I was not worthy. His immediate response was, "None of us are worthy." So how could I refuse? I had been called to serve.

Every time I serve as a Eucharistic Minister, I know that I am in the presence of God. Time is meaningless. I am only aware of the body and blood of Christ, and that he has healed me and made me worthy to stand in his presence.–Virginia

Virginia grew up in a strict Protestant tradition with a clear and deep understanding of prayer, the bible and tithing. A half dozen years ago she entered the Roman Catholic Church through the rite of Christian Initiation of adults.

Now, as indicated above, she is a commissioned extraordinary minister of Holy Communion and the elected president of our Parish Pastoral Council. Virginia also chairs the Board of Directors for a Neighborhood Faith Center which offers pastoral care to people in a center city area, most of whom are Afro-American with various needs.

Each chapter of this little book will begin with a similar quote from different extraordinary ministers of Holy Communion, testimonies that reflect their faith in the Eucharist.

When the pastoral associate at our Cathedral welcomes visitors into her office, she excitedly points out two crystals suspended next to outside windows. One of them is called a Rainbow Maker and includes a small solar panel, a suction cup for attachment to the window, and a tiny battery-operated motor that rotates the genuine crystal hanging below it. When the sun is shining and strikes the solar panel, the motor starts up and then the rotating crystal will "create beautiful rainbows that move around the room." However, when the sun hides behind clouds or the motor fails to function, the colorful spots do not appear in her office.

We have something of a parallel here with our understanding of the Eucharist. It is, of course, a major mystery of the Cathedral tradition. We can never fully grasp or totally exhaust its meaning. However, by rotating the mystery, as it were, and examining the Eucharist from different angles or perspectives, we gain a richer, fuller, and more complete comprehension of that Most Blessed Sacrament. On the contrary, concentrating on only one aspect of this great mystery limits and can even distort our perception of the Eucharist.

In this book, we will rotate the eucharistic mystery and explore it from three vantage points: first as sacrifice, then as sacrament and finally as presence. We will preface such a threefold rotating examination by analyzing another connected mystery of faith: the Paschal, Passover, or Easter Mystery of Christ's coming, dying, rising, and coming again. In the last part, the book will treat several desirable inner qualities with which we greet the risen Christ as our guest and describe ways in which the Eucharist can inspire us to serve others.

Each chapter concludes with a brief, related excerpt from the most contemporary published compendium of church teaching: the *Catechism of the Catholic Church*. These words from that text appropriately launch us on our journey.

> The Eucharist is "the source and summit of the Christian life."* "The other sacraments, and indeed all ecclesiastical ministries and works of the apostolate, are bound up with the Eucharist and are oriented toward it. For in the blessed Eucharist is contained the whole spiritual good of the Church, namely Christ himself, our Pasch."** (No. 1324)

* *LG* 11.
** *PO* 5.

CHAPTER ONE
Mystery of Faith

The invitation to become an extraordinary minister of Holy Communion came at a particularly challenging time in my life. I was a new principal; I was doing doctoral research, and most challenging of all, I was trying to raise a son in his tumultuous teens. Yet, every Sunday I was strengthened by early Mass.

Being a Eucharistic Minister has meant so much to me. It has connected me to Our Lord in a very special way. It is a wordless connection, a holy intimacy that I can share with the people of the parish. The moment when I offer them the cup of the Lord's Precious Blood or place the Body of Christ in the palm of their hand is the most significant moment of their day, perhaps week. And I have the honor of being part of that with them and with our Lord. I try always to look in their eyes, to be aware of the magnitude of this sacrament for every person, to be reverent and welcoming at the same time. As I look into their faces, some old and tired, some young and anxious, I know that they, too, struggle with jobs and family and life. And as the Blessed Sacrament heals and strengthens me, it heals and strengthens them. I am honored and humbled to be a part of that.

Memorial Acclamations

After the institutional narrative and consecration during the Liturgy of the Eucharist at Mass, the priest says or sings: "Let us proclaim the mystery of faith." The people respond, ideally by singing, but also simply by reciting, one of four memorial acclamations:

> Christ has died,
> Christ is risen
> Christ will come again.
>
> Dying you destroyed our death,
> Rising you restored our life
> Lord Jesus, come in glory.
>
> When we eat this bread and drink this cup,
> We proclaim your death, Lord Jesus,
> Until you come in glory.

Lord, by your cross and resurrection
You have set us free.
You are the Savior of the world.

We term that mystery of faith, expressed in the various acclamations, the Paschal, Passover or Easter Mystery. It embraces Christ's passion, death, resurrection, and return. It recalls Jesus coming, suffering, dying, rising, and coming again. It brings to our attention the Lord's expiration at Calvary, his Easter resurrection, and his continued presence among his people.

The Paschal Mystery

Christ proclaimed and predicted that Paschal Mystery three times in the Synoptic Gospels of Matthew, Mark, and Luke. Prior to each prediction, however, Jesus encouraged his followers with a marvelous sign of divine power. Moreover, after each proclamation, the Lord warned his listeners of what they should expect or what he expected of them, if they wished to walk in his footsteps. Here are these three predictions of his Paschal Mystery, each with its preparatory marvelous sign and subsequent application.

First Prediction of the Paschal Mystery

Marvelous Sign: Multiplication of Loaves and Fishes

All four gospels carry accounts of this familiar miracle (Matt 14:13-21; Mark 6:32-44; Luke 9:10-17; John

6:1–13). A deserted place; five thousand people; late in the day; no food available; disciples with only five loaves and a couple of fish; Jesus' directive that everyone sit down in crowds of fifty; Christ, looking "up to heaven, blessed and broke them, and gave them to the disciples to set before the crowd" (Luke 9:16); all ate until they were filled; fragments left over filled twelve baskets.

Prediction

"Then he began to teach them that the Son of Man must undergo great suffering, and be rejected by the elders, the chief priests, and the scribes, and be killed, and after three days rise again" (Mark 8:31).

Lessons for Christ's Followers: Doctrine of the Cross

"Then he said to them all, 'If any want to become my followers, let them deny themselves and take up their cross daily and follow me" (Luke 9:23).

Second Prediction of the Paschal Mystery

Marvelous Sign: Transfiguration

Jesus off to a mountain for prayer; Peter, James, and John with him; while praying, Jesus' face began shining like the sun, his garments dazzling white like snow; Peter wanting to stay there and build three booths for Christ, Moses and Elijah; a cloud overshadowed them; the three apostles became terrified; a voice from the cloud:

"This is my Son, the Chosen one. Listen to Him."; the three fell to the ground in fear; Jesus came to them, laid his hand on them and said, "Get up! Don't be afraid."; Peter, James and John then saw no one but Jesus; they came down from the mountain (Matt 17:1-8; Mark 9:2-8; Luke 9:28-36).

Prediction

"The Son of Man is going to be betrayed into human hands, and they will kill him, and on the third day he will be raised" (Matt 17:22-23).

Lesson for Christ's Followers:
Against Ambition and Envy

"Then they came to Capernaum; and when he was in the house he asked them, 'What were you arguing about on the way?' But they were silent, for on the way they had argued with one another who was the greatest. He sat down, called the twelve, and said to them, 'Whoever wants to be first must be last of all and servant of all'" (Mark 9:33-35).

"Truly I tell you, unless you change and become like children, you will never enter the kingdom of heaven. Whoever becomes humble like this child is the greatest in the kingdom of heaven" (Matt 18:3-4).

Third Prediction of the Paschal Mystery

Marvelous Sign: Healing the Crowd

There were many instances in which power went forth from Christ and healed people of various diseases. In Matthew's gospel we read that after a lengthy discourse, Jesus left Galilee and came to the district of Judea across the Jordan. The gospel then states quite simply: "Large crowds followed him, and he cured them there" (Matt 19:2).

Prediction

"See, we are going up to Jerusalem, and the Son of Man will be handed over to the chief priests and scribes, and they will condemn him to death; then they will hand him over to the Gentiles to be mocked and flogged and crucified; and on the third day he will be raised" (Matt 20:18-19).

Lesson for Christ's Followers: Servants of Others

"Whoever wishes to be first among you must be your slave; just as the Son of Man came not to be served but to serve, and to give his life a ransom for many" (Matt 20:27-28).

The Eucharist and the Paschal Mystery

At every Mass we celebrate this Paschal or Passover Mystery. Each eucharistic liturgy re-presents in unbloody fashion the death of the Lord, recalls the Resurrection, offers the Risen Lord in Holy Communion to all participants, alludes to the heavenly banquet which awaits us, and speaks of Christ's coming again in glory. Moreover, in the consecrated particles reserved at the tabernacle, the glorious resurrected Christ truly dwells in our midst for prayerful adoration and as spiritual food for those who are sick, housebound, or in prison.

Catechism of the Catholic Church

By celebrating the Last Supper with his apostles in the course of the Passover meal, Jesus gave the Jewish Passover its definitive meaning. Jesus' passing over to his father by his death and Resurrection, the new Passover, is anticipated in the Supper and celebrated in the Eucharist, which fulfills the Jewish Passover and anticipates the final Passover of the Church in the glory of the kingdom. (No. 1340)

CHAPTER TWO
Sacrifice

What an awesome privilege and honor to serve our Blessed Lord as an extraordinary Eucharistic Minister. When I look upon the host I see my Lord's crucified head with his crown of thorns. I know he died for our sins and how forgiving he is.

During my illness, it was our Beloved Lord who gave me faith. When receiving him, I know he is with me, with his love and caring—and a hug.

The Passion of the Christ

Mel Gibson's 2004 film, *The Passion of the Christ*, prompted countless controversial commentaries and attracted huge crowds in cinemas throughout the United

States. Was it a well-made motion picture? Most critics judged it so. For example, our local newspaper film reviewer gave the movie four stars out of four.

Were there violent scenes in it? Yes, brutal and prolonged violence. But crucifixion in those days of the Roman Empire was in fact a most degrading and painful death penalty. An often quoted, but anonymous remark from the Vatican summarized that particular observation about the movie in these words: "It is as it was."

Did the film move viewers' hearts? Many were touched deeply. Those already with a relationship to Christ found it powerful and inspiring. Furthermore, as a unique example of its power to move some in the audience, three high school seniors—one Protestant, one Jewish, and one atheist—all wept during the movie.

Could it be labeled anti-Semitic? While most commentators agreed that it was not blatantly or directly anti-Jewish, still some thought that the movie could sow seeds of hatred, especially in Europe.

Was there a connection in the film between Jesus' suffering and ourselves? Yes. In defending his film against accusations of anti-Semitism, Gibson argued that Christ died for our sins, for the sins of people past, present, and future. We, he maintains, are the ones who really nailed Jesus to the cross, not the Jewish leaders or even the Roman soldiers. This line of thought looks to biblical texts for support, phrases like: "Crushed for our iniquities,...by his bruises we were healed" (Isa 53:5), and "when Christ had offered for all time a single sacrifice for sins, 'he sat down at the right hand of God'" (Heb 10:12).

Moreover, experiencing the film could enhance appreciation of Jesus' love for us, what he endured for our sake. We have, as Christians, tended to sanitize the sufferings and death of the Savior. We may have read the gospel accounts, meditated upon the Passion, and prayed the Stations of the Cross. But this motion picture might *move* us more profoundly, touch us very emotionally, and cause us to truly feel in the depths of our being the agony of Calvary.

Mass and the Paschal Mystery

As we concluded in the last chapter, every Mass celebrates the Paschal or Passover Mystery. We travel from Holy Thursday through Good Friday to Easter Sunday. In each Eucharist, we recall the Last Supper, we present in unbloody fashion the Lord's death on Calvary, and we celebrate Jesus' triumph in his Resurrection. A eucharistic liturgy is both a sacrifice and a sacrament as well as a sacred action that consecrates elements reserved in the tabernacle for later prayer and distribution to the sick.

In this chapter we focus on the Eucharist as sacrifice. In the following two chapters we will rotate our attention to the same reality, first as sacrament, then as presence.

Eucharistic Prayer

We currently have more than a dozen eucharistic prayers approved for use in the United States: Eucharistic Prayers I–IV, two for reconciliation, three for children, and four from the Swiss Synod for various needs and occasions. However, every one of these texts follows the same basic format and includes identical ingredients. An outline of that pattern and an explanation of certain elements should bring out this sacrifice notion of the Eucharist.

The basic format:

- *Giving thanks.* We see the thanksgiving motif especially in the preface, during which the priest cites a specific reason for our gratitude (a feast, season, or event).
- *Acclamation.* The "Holy, holy, holy Lord...," or *Sanctus.*
- *Epiclesis or invocation of the Holy Spirit.* That prayer asks the Holy Spirit to transform bread and wine into the Body and Blood of Christ and likewise to transform spiritually all those gathered for this particular Eucharist.
- *Institution Narrative and Consecration.* Here a priest recounts and re-presents the Last Supper.
- *Anamnesis.* This Greek word means "remembrance" or "calling to mind." Following Jesus' command, "Do this in memory of me," we recall not only the Last Supper, but all of God's blessings—past, present, and what we hope for in the future.
- *Offering.* One of the reasons that the Mass is our most powerful Catholic prayer is that we offer in it not merely human petitions, but the spotless victim, the divine Christ, to the Father. In addition, at this point of the Eucharistic

Prayer we offer our own lives in union with Jesus to the Father.

- *Intercessions for the living and the dead.*
- *The final doxology.* The priest and people give all glory and honor to the Almighty Father forever and ever.

Sacrifice

The following explanations from the *Roman Missal* make explicit this notion of sacrifice:

- In the institution narrative and consecration "by means of words and action of Christ, the Sacrifice is carried out which Christ himself instituted at the Last Supper" (No. 9 d).
- "The Church's intention, however, is that the faithful not only offer this spotless victim but also learn to offer themselves" (No. 79 f).
- All the Church's members, living and dead, have "been called to participate in the redemption and salvation purchased by Christ's Body and Blood" (No. 79 g).

The Passover Event—Hebrew Scriptures

It is not possible to grasp fully the Paschal Mystery element in the Mass without recalling the Passover event so central to Jewish tradition. That story begins in the Old or First Testament, often today termed, instead, the Hebrew Scriptures. There, the Book of Exodus describes the plight of the Chosen People in pagan bondage under an unfriendly Egyptian king. God raises up Moses as their leader who confronts Pharaoh and demands that he, "Let my people go" (5:1).

The King resists and remains obdurate despite many divine signs. Finally, God directs Moses to have every family secure a year-old male lamb without blemish and to keep it until the fourteenth day in the first month of the year. Then, with loins girt, sandals on their feet, and staff in hand, they are to eat the lamb and apply some of its blood to the two doorposts and lintels of every house. The Lord told Moses and Aaron, "It is the passover of the LORD," and on that same night, "I will pass through the land of Egypt that night, and I will strike down every first-born in the land of Egypt, both human beings and animals" (12:1–12).

When the event took place, the Lord passing over the blood-marked homes and destroying the first-born in the unmarked houses, Pharaoh finally relented and let the Jewish people leave Egypt for the Promised Land. However, God, through Moses, told the people that they must remember this event perpetually with an annual ritual which recalls the unleavened bread and the spotless lamb with its saving blood. When children ask: "What does this rite mean?," the repeated reply will be: "It is the passover sacrifice to the Lord, for he passed over the houses of the Israelites in Egypt" (12:21–27).

The Passover Event—Christian Scriptures

In the New or Second Testament, often today called the Christian Scriptures, we note explicit connections between that liberating Passover event and Christ's saving death.

At the beginning of his public ministry, Jesus walked toward John the Baptist, who pointed to Christ and exclaimed: "Here is the Lamb of God who takes away the sin of the world" (John 1:29).

In the gospel account of the Last Supper, Luke clearly links this final meal of Christ with his apostles to the Passover rite. Jesus makes that connection, reinterpreting the Passover by setting it in the context of the Kingdom of God. Jesus announced to his apostles: "This cup that is poured out for you is the new covenant in my blood" (Luke 22:14–20).

On the cross, a soldier thrust his lance into Christ's side, "and at once blood and water came out" (John 19:34).

The letter to the Hebrews comments that if the blood of goats and bulls had the power to sanctify in the Jewish tradition, "how much more will the blood of Christ, who through the eternal Spirit offered himself without blemish to God, purify our conscience from dead works to worship the living God!" (9:11–14).

The First Letter of Peter instructs believers to realize "that you were ransomed from the futile ways inherited from your ancestors, not with perishable things like silver or gold, but with the precious blood of Christ, like that of a lamb without defect or blemish" (1:18-19).

In the First Letter of John, the author teaches us that "the blood of Jesus his Son cleanses us from all sin" (1:7).

Paschal, Passover, Easter

The root meaning of the word "Pasch" is "passing over," "to pass over," or "a passing over." The primary notion of the term refers to the Passover in Jewish history, but its relation to the Christian Passover should now be evident. Christ's sacrifice, this spotless Lamb of God, this perfect Victim pouring out his Blood on the Cross enables followers to pass over from spiritual death to life, from darkness to light, from sin to grace. Thus the phrases Paschal, Passover, or Easter Mystery are essentially interchangeable.

Believing and Praying

What we believe as Roman Catholics impacts how we worship. An ancient saying states that the law or way of believing *(lex credendi)* and the law or way of praying *(lex orandi)* are intimately related. Consequently, the words and actions of our worship speak to us about the truths of our faith. A few samples from the current texts and rubrics or regulations of the *Roman Missal* will confirm the mystery of the Eucharist as sacrifice and the Passover background of the Mass, plus the dominant themes of the Blood of Christ and Jesus as the Lamb of God.

Words

The Catholic Church in the West used Eucharistic Prayer I, also known as the Roman Canon, exclusively for the celebration of Mass from 1570 until 1970. Then, following the directives of the Second Vatican Council, Pope Paul VI issued a *Revised Roman Missal*. It included Eucharistic Prayer I, but added three additional ones (II, III, and IV). Subsequently, as we noted earlier, the Church has approved further eucharistic prayers for use in the United States.

We cite here passages from Eucharistic Prayer I, although similar supportive texts from those other formulas could be quoted.

The Eucharist as Sacrifice

"Through him we ask you to accept and bless
these gifts we offer you in sacrifice."

"We offer you this sacrifice of praise
for ourselves and those who are dear to us."

"...and from the many gifts you have given us
we offer you, God of glory and majesty,
this holy and perfect sacrifice:
the bread of life
and the cup of eternal salvation."

"Look with favor on these offerings
and accept them as once you accepted...
the sacrifice of Abraham our father in faith..."

"Almighty God,
we pray that your angel may take this sacrifice
to your altar in heaven."

The Passover Event and the Blood of Christ

"Take this, all of you, and drink from it:
this is the cup of my blood,
the blood of the new and everlasting covenant.
It will be shed for you and for all
so that sins may be forgiven.
Do this in memory of me."

"Father, we celebrate the memory of Christ,
    your Son.
We, your people and your ministers,
recall his passion,
his resurrection from the dead,
and his ascension into glory;"

"Then, as we receive from this altar
the sacred body and blood of your Son,
let us be filled with every grace and blessing."

Christ the Lamb of God

At the Breaking of the Bread

"Lamb of God, you take away the sins of the
    world:
have mercy on us..."

"Lamb of God, you take away the sins of the
    world:
grant us peace..."

At Communion

"This is the Lamb of God
who takes away the sins of the world,
Happy are those who are called to his supper."

Actions

The Church also employs various actions to communicate the meaning and importance of the Mass, especially the Liturgy of the Eucharist.

In the United States we *kneel* from the singing or
the recitation of the "Holy, Holy, Holy Lord...." until after
the Great Amen just prior to the Our Father. That posture
should express and deepen within us an attitude of adoration or awe during the sacred event we are experiencing.
Such a gesture and spirit mirrors the action of Muslim people. Five times daily they kneel on the floor turned toward
Mecca and bend their foreheads to the ground as they
recite the required prayers to Allah, their beneficent, merciful, one, divine, transcendent, omnipotent God.
However, this extended kneeling also conveys a notion that
the entire eucharistic prayer to a certain extent consecrates
or transforms the bread and wine into Christ's Body and
Blood. It thus enables us to offer the victorious Savior in
our midst to the Father under the guidance of the Holy
Spirit.

The Third Typical Edition of the *Roman Missal* directs that "a little before the consecration, when appropriate, a server rings a *bell* as a signal to the faithful" (No. 150). This generally occurs at what is termed the epiclesis, an action in which the priest extends his hands over the bread and wine, asking the Holy Spirit to make them the Body and Blood of Christ. While reciting these words, the presiding priest also traces a sign of the cross over those two elements.

That gesture—the *laying on of hands*—recalls numerous incidents in the New Testament at which Jesus and others laid their hands upon people for healing the sick, blessing children, or setting individuals aside for assigned tasks. It also mirrors a Jewish tradition when the priest on a special day of repentance laid hands upon an animal, the "scapegoat," symbolizing the transmission of all sins to this creature. He then sent the scapegoat out into the desert, into oblivion, thus removing the people's transgressions and casting them into forgetfulness. The connection of this scapegoat with Christ, the Lamb of God, the victim whose sacrificial gift on the cross makes forgiveness and forgetfulness of our sins possible, should be clear.

The church highlights in a unique way the Institutional Narrative and Words of Consecration. For example, it requires in the official altar prayer book, *The Sacramentary*, a slightly *larger type* for the actual words of Jesus. "Take this...and eat it," "Take this...and drink from it." Regulations or rubrics also direct the priest to bow his head slightly as he pronounces these phrases. Nevertheless, the American bishops caution that the priest should still proclaim this narrative as one continuous prayer of thanksgiving and blessing, an integral part of the entire eucharistic prayer.

We will now rotate this mystery of the Eucharist to examine it as sacrament.

Catechism of the Catholic Church

The Eucharist is called the "Memorial of the Lord's Passion and Resurrection." It is also termed:

> The *Holy Sacrifice,* because it makes present the one sacrifice of Christ the Savior and includes the Church's offering. The terms *holy sacrifice of the Mass,* "*sacrifice of praise,*" *spiritual sacrifice, pure and holy sacrifice* are also used,* since it completes and surpasses all the sacrifices of the Old Covenant. (No. 1330)

---

* *Heb* 13:15; cf. *1 Pet* 2:5; *Ps* 116:13, 17; *Mal* 1:11.

CHAPTER THREE
Sacrament

*T*he portrait of the Infant Jesus carried lovingly by St. Anthony inspired me to pray for the special grace of someday (hopefully in heaven) carrying the Infant Jesus too. This prayer was answered in an unexpected way when I volunteered to be a Eucharistic Minister. I realized that in this awesome role I have my God enthroned in my hands even only for a few brief moments. These are moments of immense love and immense happiness beyond all telling.

Several years ago an eye specialist announced to my brother: "Friend, you are now legally blind because of macular degeneration." He has partial sight, but can no longer read or drive a car.

Both are, naturally, frustrating developments. The former, in particular, hurts the most because my brother's entire professional life has revolved around reading, viewing, and writing as a book reviewer, film critic, and newspaper editor. Those tasks are no longer possible. Moreover, someone, usually his spouse of fifty plus years, must read for him daily mail, the newspaper, and restaurant menus.

Nevertheless, with partial eyesight he can see things in general, blurred fashion; walk unaided; and take long plane trips with little difficulty. Still, at airports, he wishes that the stick signs indicating restrooms for men would be larger so he would know where he is going.

That is what signs do. They point to something beyond, something we cannot see. Arrows and words on major highways tell us where exit ramps will take us; shrill sirens warn us about approaching emergency vehicles; sour smells from milk containers indicate that their contents have passed the expiration date printed on the bottle cap or cardboard carton.

Signs are sensible objects: we can see, smell, hear, feel, even taste them. They give us knowledge of something beyond those external signs. Human beings have developed many or most signs, like the exit ramp words and arrows or the shrill sirens of emergency vehicles. Nature has given us others, like smoke, which indicates a fire, or thunder, an approaching storm.

With our wonderful, God-given minds we can move past human or material signs to realities suggested by them.

Symbols

Some, but not all, signs are also symbols. Signs communicate knowledge of something beyond, but they generally do not move us emotionally or stir our hearts. Signs that are symbols do. They possess a remarkable, often unconscious power to touch, motivate, and inspire.

- A circular ring on the third finger, left hand signifies: "I am married." Gently rubbed while awaiting serious surgery, the same ring, in symbolic fashion, stimulates thoughts such as "Someone loves me, cares about me, will be by my side throughout this struggle."
- The championship trophy a hockey player holds high while skating around the rink, signifies a team won the title. But the symbolic trophy and the celebration simultaneously generate pride, gratitude, and joy.
- A crude American flag in a Vietnamese prison signifies the United States of America. But to those service personnel incarcerated there for several years, a joint pledge of allegiance before that hand-made symbol at 4:00 p.m. every afternoon stirs within them strength, hope, and courage.

Sacraments

The seven Roman Catholic sacraments are signs and usually symbols as well. They point beyond, but often also move our hearts. In the older, traditional definition of sacraments, the Church declares that they are outward signs, instituted by Christ and designed to bestow grace.

As *outward signs*, bread, water, wine, oil, hands, and words are all sensible objects, things we can perceive with our senses. Moreover, they point to spiritual realities beyond that which we outwardly experience: the new life received in baptism, for example; or the Risen Lord's Body and Blood in the Eucharist; or the healing power in the anointing of the sick.

The sacraments have been *instituted by Christ* who entrusted them to the Church. There is explicit mention of some sacraments in the sacred scriptures. Thus, at the very end of Matthew's gospel, Jesus commanded his apostles: "Go therefore and make disciples of all nations, baptizing them in the name of the Father and of the Son and of the Holy Spirit" (Matt 28:19). We have another illustration in the letter of James: "Are any among you sick? They should call for the elders of the church and have them pray over them, anointing them with oil in the name of the Lord" (Jas 5:14). There is still a third instance in John's gospel, where Jesus teaches: "So Jesus said to them, '...unless you eat the flesh of the Son of Man and drink his blood, you have no life in you'" (John 6:53).

God established these sacraments *to give, bestow,* or *dispense grace*. That includes, first, sanctifying grace or the life of the Risen Christ within us; next, special graces to live out the responsibilities connected with each sacrament; and finally, a unique permanent character in three sacraments (baptism, confirmation, holy orders) to assist us in fulfilling the particular missions or responsibilities of baptized and confirmed Christians as well as deacons, priests, or bishops.

While all of the sacraments bestow the grace of Christ, the Eucharist does something more. It makes present and gives us Jesus himself, or, in the words of the *Catholic Catechism, "the whole Christ is truly, really and substantially contained"* within the consecrated bread and wine (No. 1374).

In a certain sense, every sacrament leads to or flows from the Eucharist. The initiation sacraments of baptism and confirmation makes us members of the Church and thus eligible to receive the Eucharist in Communion. When serious sin cuts us off from the Church and the Eucharist, penance, reconciliation, or confession brings us back to both so that we may appropriately receive Holy Communion. Anointing of the sick restores ill persons to health, enabling them to rejoin the believing community at Mass. Holy Orders ordains priests who can celebrate Mass. Ideally, we celebrate matrimony within a eucharistic service, the Mass.

The Mystery of the Mass

The Mass is a spiritual, invisible mystery, but still made up of two material, visible parts: the Liturgy of the Word and the Liturgy of the Eucharist. In addition, there are brief introductory and concluding rites.

We can describe the movement of those liturgies quite simply in terms of two mountains, each with ascending and descending slopes, leading to and flowing from God.

In the Liturgy of the Word, we, as it were, speak to God (Penitential Rite, Gloria, Opening Prayer, Responsorial Psalm, Creed, and General Intercessions). God in response speaks to us (the three biblical readings and a Spirit-inspired homily).

In the Liturgy of the Eucharist, we, as it were, give to God (gifts presented and transformed, then offered to the Father through Christ in the Holy Spirit). God in response gives to us (Jesus' Body and Blood in Communion).

Having been fed by the Word and Sacrament, we are sent out from Mass to bring the Good News to others in the world around us.

Manna from Heaven

After the Chosen People had fled from the slavery of Egypt and been delivered by God's protective power through the waters of the Red Sea, they encamped in the desert of Sin en route to the promised land. However, they quickly forgot how the mighty Lord had freed them and grumbled to Moses and Aaron about their condition. "If only we had died by the hand of the Lord in the land of Egypt, when we sat by the fleshpots and ate our fill of bread" (Exod 16:3).

God responded to those complaints and told Moses: "I am going to rain bread from heaven for you, and each day the people shall go out and gather enough for that day....On the sixth day, when they prepare what they bring in, it will be twice as much as they gather on other days" (Exod 16:4–5). That miraculous daily bread later came to be called "manna" and was seen as God's gift of coming down from the sky.

Bread of Life

The sixth chapter of John's gospel begins with two marvelous deeds: the multiplication of the loaves and fishes, then Jesus walking on the water and reassuring the frightened disciples by saying, "It is I; do not be afraid" (John 6:1-21).

These two miracles prepared Christ's followers for his subsequent discourse in that chapter about the Bread of Life. The disciples, still struggling with doubts, asked for a sign that would help them believe. They reminded Jesus, "Our ancestors ate the manna in the wilderness; as it is written, 'He gave them bread from heaven to eat'" (6:31).

Christ responded to their questions and request with these words: "I am the bread of life. Whoever comes to me will never be hungry, and whoever believes in me will never be thirsty" (6:35). When many continued to murmur about this teaching, Jesus reiterated his message and expanded upon it:

> I am the bread of life. Your ancestors ate the manna in the wilderness, and they died. This is the bread that comes down from heaven, so that one may eat of it and not die. I am the living bread that came

down from heaven. Whoever eats of this
bread will live for ever. (6:48-51)

Christ then goes on to make this more explicitly
clear.

Those who eat my flesh and drink my
blood have eternal life, and I will raise
them up on the last day; for my flesh is
true food and my blood is true
drink....This is the bread that came down
from heaven, not like that which your
ancestors ate, and they died. But the one
who eats this bread will live for ever.
(6:54-55, 58)

Communion Rite

In the Communion Rite, God feeds us with this
bread of life. It begins with the *Our Father*, which is a nat-
ural bridge from the "We Give to God" movement to the
"God Gives to Us" slope. The first petitions address
God; the second set of petitions speak of our needs.
"Give us this daily bread" refers to all our everyday neces-
sities, but also points to the bread from heaven we are
about to receive. When we prepare for Holy Communion,
whether within or outside Mass, the Church's liturgy
always includes the Our Father for the reasons we have
just mentioned.

The *sign of peace* follows: "Let us offer each other
the sign of peace." There is a double meaning to this ges-

ture, an action meant to be more of a serious reconciliation effort, than a mere lively reunion of friends. First, it applies practically to the latter part of the Our Father: "Forgive us our trespasses as we forgive those who trespass against us." Secondly, it also prepares us for the oneness or unity that should be present as we, though many, receive the same one Risen Christ in Communion.

Words that accompany the *mixing* of a broken *consecrated particle* with the *Precious Blood*, even though said quietly by the priest, explain that action so rich in symbolism: "May this mingling of the body and blood of Christ bring eternal life to us who receive it."

The *priest's proclamation and invitation* springs from John the Baptist's announcement at the beginning of Jesus' public ministry: "This is the Lamb of God who takes away the sins of the world" (John 1:29). It also refers to the Book of Revelation (19:9): "Blessed are those who are invited to the marriage supper of the Lamb." The liturgical invitation, of course, is slightly different: "Happy are those who are called to his supper."

In response to that invitation, the people present respond in words that recall the centurion's urgent plea to Jesus as he begged the Lord to cure his paralyzed servant who was "suffering dreadfully" at home. The soldier humbled himself before Christ and said: "Lord, I am not worthy to have you come under my roof; but only speak the word, and my servant will be healed." (Matt 8:5-8).

Our response at Mass is, again, similar, yet different: "Lord, I am not worthy to receive you, but only say the word and I shall be healed."

Reverence

In approaching such an awesome mystery, the gift of the Risen Lord himself, we express with several reverent gestures our inner faith and respect. For the first Christian millennium, communicants received the consecrated bread in their hands. In doing so, they were instructed to make a throne of their outstretched palms to receive the Eucharistic King, being very careful not to drop any particles. During the second millennium, for various reasons, the custom prevailed of receiving hosts directly on the tongue and communicants generally approaching the altar with folded hands. In this third millennium, it would seem that both procedures, in the hand or on the tongue, will be options for most Roman Catholics.

The publication of the *General Instruction of the Roman Missal, Third Edition*, with adaptations approved by our American Bishops, has made standing the norm for reception of Holy Communion in the dioceses of the United States. Nevertheless, persons who kneel should not be denied Communion. It also directs communicants to bow their heads slightly in reverence when they come before the minister who is distributing to them the Body of the Lord or the Precious Blood.

To reflect our belief that Christ remains within us for a period of time after Communion, linking us with himself and with others, we join in a hymn of grateful praise or pause a few moments for silent reflection.

Effects of the Sacrament

The great theologian and doctor of the Church, St. Thomas Aquinas, published in the Middle Ages his famous *Summa Theologica*. In Part III, Question 79 and Article 2, he succinctly summarizes the effect of this sacrament, Holy Communion, given by way of food and drink. That sacrament, according to St. Thomas, does for one's spiritual life all that material food does for the bodily life.

Thus, Holy Communion

- *Sustains us.* An ancient proverb reminds all that we eat to live, not live to eat. Regular and appropriate eating habits are essential for good health. Conversely, those who overeat or undereat eventually encounter some form of illness. In parallel fashion, frequent reception of the Eucharist maintains and nourishes our spiritual life; neglecting Holy Communion can, on the contrary, damage and even destroy our spiritual life.

- *Increases our life.* Parents marvel at how rapidly infants and children grow. Holy Communion similarly strengthens, nourishes, and deepens the life of Christ within us.

- *Restores our life.* One of the immediate resources for emergency room personnel in treating a seriously ill patient is the insertion of an intravenous tube. Dehydration and lack of nourishment cause serious complications; food and drink supplied in this fashion help restore the ill person to health. When our spiritual life weakens or fails, this sacrament likewise brings us back and rebuilds our inner life.

- *Delights us.* When we are very thirsty after vigorous exercise or extremely hungry at the end of a long work day, a cold water fountain or favorite dish can bring us great joy. Holy Communion also invariably fills us with a deep sense of well being and inner serenity.

Having examined two dimensions of the eucharistic mystery—as sacrifice and sacrament—we will now explore it as presence, consecrated hosts reserved for the homebound sick and our prayerful adoration.

Catechism of the Catholic Church

In the communion, preceded by the Lord's prayer and the breaking of the bread, the faithful receive "the bread of heaven" and "the cup of salvation," the body and blood of Christ who offered himself "for the life of the world."* (No. 1355)

---

* Jn 6:51.

CHAPTER FOUR
Presence

*F*ather, I stood like a child, in feeling and posture, on my first day administering the Eucharist. The feeling was overwhelming. I tried to be very cautious and alert as I felt I simply could not make a mistake. I also felt quite reverent, as if God had put me here, in this Cathedral, at this time, to do a very important job. To be his servant and to serve others in this precious and most sacred way. What a privilege to be a modern day lay minister and in so doing strengthening my understanding and appreciation of our faith. I am most grateful but also undeserving. May Christ grant me the grace to continue in my journey back to him.

A Brief History

The Church from earliest days has believed that the Risen Christ becomes truly, really, and substantially present during the words of institution or consecration at Mass. It also maintains that this Presence of Jesus continues in the consecrated species for a period of time afterwards. The brief and simplified history of devotion to that Eucharistic Presence which follows should illustrate how this faith has impacted the daily life of Catholic Christians.

In initial years, believers took some of the consecrated particles home for distribution to the sick or to prisoners. There were, of course, no churches or tabernacles in those first three centuries of persecution. Moreover, while there was great reverence for the Eucharist, we can discover no pattern of people kneeling in adoration and prayer before the Blessed Sacrament as we do today.

During the fourth century, with its legalization of Christianity, churches multiplied. So did a spiritual practice called the "composition of place," in which Christians sought to situate themselves consciously in the presence of God. To help achieve that composition of place, people made pilgrimages to the Holy Land and to Jerusalem specifically. Others found the newly constructed churches preferred places for private prayer, particularly before an altar or cross.

From the sixth to the twelfth centuries, a gradual change occurred in locating the reserved Blessed Sacrament: from the home, to the sacristy or interior vesting area of the church, to a receptacle or tabernacle upon, above, or near the altar. During the twelfth through the fourteenth centuries, the practice of devotion to the Blessed Sacrament, usually in a tabernacle upon the altar, grew rapidly. Extra candles, genuflections, a locked and secure tabernacle, processions, the feast of Corpus Christi with prayers composed by St. Thomas Aquinas, the example of St. Francis Assisi, the forty hour service, an exposed consecrated host—all these became commonplace in Catholic life. Those elements would continue to dominate the devotional life of Roman Catholics until the middle of the twentieth century.

Contemporary Shifts

Countless Catholics over the centuries found these devotions attractive because they expressed their faith in the Lord's Eucharistic Real Presence; were understandable, often celebrated in the vernacular language; and facilitated active participation. On the other hand, Masses during those days were usually in Latin; lay persons tended to be silent spectators; and participation was limited to Holy Communion with not all, or even most, individuals coming forward to receive the Eucharist.

Liturgical reforms in the 1900s altered that situation. During the first decade, Pope Pius X encouraged early and frequent Holy Communion. Starting in the second half of that century, the Church greatly mitigated fasting before Communion; most Masses were now celebrated in the vernacular; rubrics called for active participation by all lay persons present; and priests offered the Eucharist at more convenient times, including late afternoon or early evening hours. Eucharistic devotions did not disappear, but their popularity greatly declined.

In 1973, the Roman Congregation for Divine Worship issued the document *Eucharistic Worship Outside Mass*. It praised this type of devotion and provided various services involving the Eucharist, but also clarified the relationship between those devotions and the Mass as sacrifice and sacrament.

These two paragraphs from a Decree introducing this document summarize that clarification:

> The celebration of the eucharist in the sacrifice of the Mass is the true origin and purpose of the worship shown to the eucharist outside Mass. The principle reason for reserving the sacrament after Mass is to unite, through sacramental communion, the faithful unable to participate in the Mass, especially the sick and the aged, with Christ and the offering of his sacrifice.
>
> In turn, eucharistic reservation, which became customary in order to permit the reception of communion, led to the practice of adoring this sacrament and offering to it the worship which is due to God. This cult of adoration is based upon valid and solid principles. Moreover, some of

the public and communal forms of this worship were instituted by the Church itself.

Three practical directives dramatize this teaching about the correct relationship between eucharistic devotions and the Mass:

First, only a single genuflection is made in the presence of the Blessed Sacrament, whether reserved in the tabernacle or exposed for public adoration. The custom prior to that was a double genuflection—on both knees—before the exposed sacrament. That in effect says that the exposed consecrated host ranks higher and deserves more respect than the sacrifice of the Mass from which it has its origin.

Second, for exposition of the Blessed Sacrament in the monstrance, only four to six candles are lighted, as at Mass. Again, a prior custom would have two candelabra, each with at least a half dozen lighted candles. That proclaims the same message as the double genuflection.

Third, the ritual issues this caution: "When the faithful honor Christ present in the sacrament, they should remember that this presence is derived from the sacrament and is directed toward sacramental and spiritual communion" (No. 80).

In 1992, the U.S. Bishops Committee on the Liturgy issued the *Order for the Solemn Exposition of the Holy Eucharist.*

We will now discuss several of these revised and up-to-date eucharistic devotions, including those covered by that 1992 ritual about solemn exposition.

Communion Outside of Mass

Bringing Holy Communion to the sick was a major pastoral task for parish clergy prior to the 1960s and 1970s. Priests usually had a list of sick or elderly housebound persons (mine at one parish contained 75 names) and faithfully visited them at least once a month, bringing consecrated hosts.

Two developments in 1973 both slightly and radically changed that pattern. A new rite published in response to the directives of the Second Vatican Council contained a richer ritual for Communion Outside of Mass, especially to the sick. This included the Our Father, pertinent biblical readings, and active participation in the prayers by the sick or housebound and their caregivers. That was fundamentally a slight or minor change.

In that same year, Pope Paul VI approved special or extraordinary ministers of Holy Communion, a decree to be included in the ritual we have just described. These were necessary to assist the clergy with distribution of Holy Communion at weekend Masses. However, these ministers were also empowered to bring Holy Communion to the sick and homebound. This was essentially a radical and major change.

A swift implementation of that decree meant that within a decade extraordinary ministers of Holy Communion in the United States numbered in the hundreds of thousands. Many of them began to carry the Eucharistic Lord to those confined at home on a more frequent basis, even on Sundays. Such a desired Sabbath practice was not then, and is not now, physically feasible for parish priests.

A 1983 ritual book for the United States, *Pastoral Care of the Sick*, reflects that rapid and widespread development. It states that priests with pastoral responsibilities should arrange for the sick or aged, even though not seriously ill or in danger of death, to be given opportunities for Holy Communion frequently, even daily, especially during the Easter season and particularly on Sundays. Parish priests still need to visit those housebound persons as their spiritual shepherds as well as to minister to them the sacraments of Penance and Anointing of the Sick.

Holy Cross Church in Vero Beach on Florida's east coast illustrates this new procedure. At several of the Sunday Masses a few extraordinary ministers come to the altar after Communion, each receiving from the priest a pyx or container with consecrated hosts. The presiding clergy person then addresses the congregation and those ministers of mercy to the sick in this fashion:

> Let us ask the Lord to look with kindness
> on these Ministers of Holy Communion
> who have been instructed to bring the
> life-giving Body and Blood of Christ to
> the sick and housebound members of the
> parish....May you go in peace.

These ministers take with them a copy of the bulletin, read from the Sunday scriptures to the housebound, summarize the homily, follow the ritual prayers and converse with those they are visiting.

This is a near perfect scenario: it dramatizes the truth that Holy Communion flows out of and leads to the Mass; it expresses great reverence for the risen Christ present in the consecrated particle(s); it links the confined housebound persons with the healthy parishioners assembled for Mass.

Eucharistic Congresses

A Eucharistic Congress on the diocesan, national, or international level gathers people to reflect upon the meaning of the Eucharist and to honor the Blessed Sacrament with public worship. For example, in the mid 1970s, the Archdiocese of Philadelphia hosted the 41st International Eucharistic Congress.

There is a double element in spiritual events like these: extensive preparation efforts and the actual congress itself. Guidelines for the preparatory process suggest study and instruction about the Eucharist, active participation in anticipatory liturgies, and research or promotion of social justice concerns like the appropriate distribution of property. Norms for the actual Congress include celebration of the Eucharist as the center and high point; word services; conferences and meetings to explore the Congress theme; extended adoration and common prayer in the presence of the Blessed Sacrament; and eucharistic processions, where feasible.

The Philadelphia Congress attracted thousands from all over the world and culminated in a massive Mass at a huge local stadium.

Eucharistic Exposition and Adoration

As we have seen, Catholic Christians from the very beginning believed in the real presence of Christ after the consecration or institutional narrative. That faith quite naturally led to great reverence for the consecrated particles and distribution to the sick or persons in prison.

However, it was only at the start of the second millennium that members of the Church began to pray before the Blessed Sacrament. In this development, the vessel containing the consecrated particles moved to a public place in the church, either above or actually on the altar and eventually received the title of tabernacle. Then adoration and prayer before the Blessed Sacrament led to such popular devotions as exposition of and benediction with a consecrated host, the Forty Hours Devotion, and perpetual adoration of the exposed Blessed Sacrament.

The 1973 document *Eucharistic Worship Outside Mass* succinctly clarifies in the following two paragraphs the relationship between the Eucharist as Sacrifice, Sacrament, and Presence or as Mass, Communion, and Exposition:

> Exposition of the holy eucharist, either in the ciborium or in the monstrance, is intended to acknowledge Christ's marvelous presence in the sacrament. Exposi-

tion invites us to the spiritual union with him that culminates in sacramental communion. Thus it fosters very well the worship which is due to Christ in spirit and in truth.

This kind of exposition must clearly express the cult of the blessed sacrament in its relationship to the Mass. The plan of the exposition should carefully avoid anything which might somehow obscure the principal desire of Christ in instituting the eucharist, namely, to be with us as food, medicine, and comfort (No.82).

In addition to the points about a simple genuflection and the number of candles, which we have already mentioned, the ritual contains certain regulations to keep those relationships in perspective:

- At the altar where or when Mass is celebrated, there should be no reservation of the sacrament in the tabernacle from the beginning of Mass. Christ's eucharistic presence is the fruit of the consecration and should appear to be such. A later regulation in 2002 is even more direct, stating that the tabernacle should not even be on an altar at which Mass is celebrated.
- Exposition should include biblical readings, prayers, songs, and silent reflection before the blessing or benediction.

- The rubrics prohibit exposition simply for the sake of benediction only.
- The devotional exercise should match the seasons of the church year, thus in some ways flowing from the liturgy and leading people back to it.

Forty Hours Devotion

Over the past several centuries a particular form of prayer before the exposed Blessed Sacrament called the Forty Hours Devotion has been celebrated annually in churches throughout the world.

It began in the early part of the seventeenth century at the Church of the Holy Sepulchre in Milan, Italy. The forty-hour time span concept apparently grew out of an earlier tradition in which devout Christians prayed in a special way for forty hours as they recalled the interval between Jesus' body being laid in the tomb after his death on Good Friday until the resurrection at Easter. This devotion spread rather quickly throughout the church, gained official recognition universally, and was approved for all the dioceses of the United States in 1868.

While the Forty Hours Devotion may be conducted continuously, probably most churches interrupt the exposition in the evening and celebrate the event over two or three days. Church directives encourage such celebrations on an annual basis. Some dioceses even devise a schedule so that the Forty Hours Devotion is always being observed at some parish throughout the year.

The goal of this and other forms of eucharistic devotion is to call the people of God to a deeper love for the holy eucharist and a more faithful living of the Christian life. Exposition, whether in the ciborium (a vessel containing many particles) or the monstrance (an upright vessel in which the larger host used by the priest at Mass is placed in the center for visibility and adoration) should lead participants to acknowledge Jesus' marvelous presence in the sacrament and to grow in union with Christ, which culminates in Holy Communion.

Perpetual Adoration

In one eastern city a cloister of Dominican sisters prays continuously day and night before the exposed Blessed Sacrament. Of course, only several members are actually present for such adoration at a given time. Across the country, just south of San Francisco, another cloister of women religious likewise maintain perpetual adoration of the Eucharist. There are many similar religious communities throughout the United States in which perpetual adoration of the Blessed Sacrament is part of their constitutions or regulations.

Over the past decade, however, a considerable number of parishes have begun, with their bishop's approval, perpetual adoration of the Blessed Sacrament in chapels or spaces constructed specifically for this purpose. In my former parish, several hundred people signed up for a weekly hour of adoration on an around the clock basis. I always found it inspirational to stop in at any time and find a few people praying silently before Christ present in the consecrated particle. Father Tom McCread, now retired pastor of St. Francis of Assisi parish in Wichita, Kansas, credits the remarkable vibrancy of his parish to the prayers of over three hundred people who spend an hour each week in adoration of the Blessed Sacrament. Nevertheless, the Church cautions that there must always be at least two present in the chapel when there is exposition of the Blessed Sacrament.

The Tabernacle

Our brief historical sketch at the beginning of this chapter indicated that the tabernacle was a development of the Middle Ages, even being placed above or actually on the altar. Today, a millennium later, the most current church directives have this to say about the nature and placement of the tabernacle:

- It should be in a part of the church that is truly noble, prominent, readily visible, beautifully decorated, and suitable for prayer.
- This one tabernacle should be immovable, of solid and inviolable material that is not transparent.
- It should be kept locked.
- It could be in the sanctuary or in some chapel suitable for private adoration and prayer.
- A special lamp, fueled by oil or wax, should burn continuously to indicate and honor the presence of Christ.

(Note: These directives are from Nos. 314–316 of the 2002 *General Instruction of the Roman Missal*.)

Role Models

The Church in every age has members noted for their devotion to the Blessed Sacrament. St. Ignatius of Loyola, founder of the Society of Jesus, or Jesuits, is remembered as having said that should the Church suppress the community he founded, fifteen minutes before the tabernacle could give him an inner serenity in the face of such a disheartening development.

The late Archbishop Fulton J. Sheen wrote a chapter in his autobiography, *Treasure in Clay*, entitled, "The Hour That Made My Day." Sheen describes his decision, made before priesthood ordination, to spend an hour each day at prayer in front of the Blessed Sacrament. A half century later, Archbishop Sheen would say that he had fulfilled this promise or goal and often recommended the practice at many clergy conferences.

Carlo Coretto, one of the Little Brothers of Charles de Foucauld, lives a contemplative life in an African desert. He arises very early, long before daylight, and spends some time outside reflecting upon God's grandeur seen in the wonders of creation. Then he enters the small chapel where a sanctuary lamp filled with olive oil flickers before the tabernacle. This is his customary and preferred place of prayer. Why? There he feels the presence of God most strongly. There he makes his way to the threshold of the invisible and the Eucharist, for him, is the surest doorway opening to it.

St. Ignatius, Archbishop Sheen, and Brother Carlo with faith and love welcomed Christ present in the Blessed Sacrament as a guest into their hearts. We will now look at some inner qualities needed to meet or connect with the Risen Christ in the Eucharist as Sacrifice, Sacrament, or Presence, attitudes required to receive him properly as a guest into our hearts.

Catechism of the Catholic Church

The Eucharistic presence of Christ begins at the moment of the consecration and endures as long as the Eucharistic species subsist. (No. 1377)

CHAPTER FIVE
Guest

When the opportunity to be a Eucharistic Minister was offered to me, I felt a more profound door to my spiritual life was opened. Confusion and nervousness took over. I believed my hands were not worthy of touching Christ's Body and Blood. Finally, I understood that this was God's will and I was going through this door confident of becoming even closer to Our Lord and serving others in some way.

On Masses at Pentecost, the familiar Latin sequence *Veni, Sancte Spiritus* occurs after the second reading. Here are two verses from it in a poetic English version: "You, of comforters the best; You, the soul's most welcome guest." The phrases are addressed to the Holy

Spirit, but they could well be applied to the Risen Christ present in the Eucharist.

Benedictine monasteries, following the teaching of their founder, observe this norm: "When a guest comes, Christ comes." In their everyday experiences, most people make careful preparations for guests who are about to visit. They seek to practice gracious hospitality.

A parallel does or should exist in our hearts and lives when we prepare to welcome a very unique guest, the Eucharistic Jesus as sacrifice, sacrament, or presence. Some very obvious desired qualities, characteristics, or inner attitudes come to mind. We will explore these in this chapter.

Awe

When Moses came to Horeb, the mountain of God, an angel of the Lord appeared to him out of a bush which, though on fire, was not consumed. As Moses moved closely to examine this remarkable phenomenon, God called out and said, "Come no closer! Remove the sandals from your feet, for the place on which you are standing is holy ground."…"I am the God of your father, the God of Abraham, the God of Isaac, and the God of Jacob." Moses was so shaken by all this that he hid his face, for the Jewish leader feared looking at God (Exod 3:1–6).

God demanded that Moses cultivate within himself and in his exterior actions a sense of awe and wonder before the Almighty One, the Creator of heaven and earth, the totally beyond transcendent Being. Those in the Jewish tradition reflect that awe and wonder even today, wearing skull caps in their synagogues, treating the very name of God with great reverence and bowing at prayer before the Wailing Wall in Jerusalem. Those in the Muslim tradition address God as Allah, the Beneficent, the Merciful, the one, transcendent, omnipotent God; they pray five times daily in adoration and bow with their foreheads touching the ground as they do.

Those in the Catholic Christian tradition ideally possess the same awe and wonder before the divine Christ coming into our midst and remaining with us in the Eucharist. During the sacrifice of the Mass, we join in a hymn of praise, "Glory to God in the highest;" we sing "Holy, holy, holy Lord, God of power and might"; and we kneel in prayerful adoration as the Risen Jesus comes into our midst. During the sacrament of Holy Communion, we come forward with folded or outstretched hands, bow slightly toward the Eucharistic Lord held out before us, and spend a few moments in quiet prayer afterwards, conscious of the unique divine presence within our hearts. At prayer before Christ's Presence in the tabernacle, we kneel, genuflect, or bow in adoration, keep a candle burning continuously as a reminder of the Divine Guest there, and participate in special services honoring the Blessed Sacrament.

Faith

Jesus often retired to deserted places to pray. On one of those occasions, he went off on a mountain by himself and remained there alone throughout the evening.

Meanwhile, the disciples at Christ's insistence got into a boat and began their journey to the other side.

Violent wind storms arise swiftly and unexpectedly on the Sea of Galilee causing huge and dangerous waves. That was the case this night with the storm tossing about their tiny vessel.

Around three in the morning, Jesus came toward the frightened apostles walking on the water. This further terrified them. In response to their fearful cries, Christ hastened to reassure them with these words: "Take heart, it is I; do not be afraid."

Peter then asked the Lord if he could come to him across the water. Jesus said: "Come." Peter did so. But after a few steps, feeling and seeing the fierce wind, he became frightened and cried, "Lord, save me!"

Christ immediately stretched out his hand, caught him, and rebuked Peter: "You of little faith, why did you doubt?"

When they got into the boat, the wind ceased.

Those in the vessel then expressed their awe, wonder, and reverence for Jesus and declared, "Truly you are the Son of God" (Matt 14:22–33).

Faith is the basis for awe, wonder, and reverence. That divinely given inner quality enables us to look beyond our many experiences and discover the presence of God. We can look beyond beauty—a spectacular sunset, beautiful fall colors, a star-filled sky—and recognize the Creator of heaven and earth. We can look beyond positive coincidences and discover in them the protective love of a caring God. We can look beyond the biblical words proclaimed at

Mass and realize that it is Christ speaking to us. We can look beyond the familiar actions of Mass and believe that our prayers and gifts have been transformed into a perfect sacrifice, which we can offer to the Father through Christ in the Holy Sprit. We can look beyond the consecrated bread and wine and welcome within us truly the Body and Blood of Christ. We can look beyond the decorated tabernacle with the flickering candle near it and confidently pray to the Risen Christ inside reserved for our adoration and for the sick.

Gratitude

When Jesus was passing along the borders of Samaria and Galilee, ten lepers came out from their village to meet him. Leprosy, a hideous disease without the remedies of our times, was considered to be contagious and an affliction that also rendered the victim ritually unclean. Thus, lepers faced the ravages of this illness, isolation from all people, and religious rejection. The afflicted lepers consequently kept their distance from Christ, but still raised their voices and pleaded: "Jesus, Master, have mercy on us!" As they left him, the ten eventually recognized that they had been cured of their terrible affliction. One, realizing that he had been totally healed, returned, praising God in a loud voice, and threw himself on his face at the feet of Jesus. The Master replied: "Were not ten made clean? But the other nine, where are they? Was none of them found to return and give praise to God except this foreigner?" (Luke 17:11–18).

If we, with wonder and faith, view everything as a gift from God, then a spirit of gratitude naturally flows from that vision. The Jewish scriptures, the Old or First Testament, contain rich prayers expressing our gratefulness. For example, Psalm 136's central and recurrent theme is "Give thanks to the Lord, for he is good, for his mercy endures forever." The Book of Daniel contains the famous song of three young men in the fiery furnace which blesses or praises and, in effect, thanks the Lord for many gifts: "Bless the Lord, all you works of the Lord, praise and exalt him above all forever" (Dan 3:57 NAB). These works include such elements as shower and dew, frost and chill, ice and snow, lightning and clouds, seas and rivers.

As a devout Jewish person, Jesus would have frequently, over one hundred times a day, praised God for the many gifts he was experiencing at that very moment—sun, air, food, water, a mother's love. He also explicitly broke into a hymn of thanks at one moment in his public ministry: Jesus rejoiced in the Holy Spirit and said: "I thank you, Father, Lord of heaven and earth, because you have hidden these things from the wise and the intelligent and have revealed them to infants" (Luke 10:21).

However, it was at the Last Supper that we see most significantly Christ expressing thanks. The three gospel accounts and St. Paul's description of that event in his First Letter to the Corinthians give us these familiar words: "Then he took a cup, and after giving thanks" and "Then he took a loaf of bread, and when he had given thanks, he broke it" (Matt 26:26-29; Mark 14:22-25; Luke 22:14-20; 1 Cor 11:17-34).

In Mass, during the Liturgy of the Eucharist, at the institutional narrative, or consecration, the Church replicates what Jesus said and did at the Last Supper:

> Before he was given up to death,
> a death he freely accepted,
> he took bread and gave you thanks.
>
> When supper was ended, he took the cup.
> Again he gave you thanks and praise...
> (Eucharistic Prayer II)

The priest creates this climate of gratitude just prior to those words in the dialogue of the Preface: "Let us give thanks to the Lord our God." The people respond by saying that it is right to give God thanks and praise.

The priest continues with the standard beginning of the Preface: "Father, all-powerful and ever-living God, we do well always and everywhere to give you thanks through Jesus Christ our Lord."

That gratitude motif continues after the consecration or institutional narrative. In Eucharistic Prayer III, the priest, speaking in our name, uses these words: "We offer you in thanksgiving this holy and living sacrifice."

The Greek root of the very word "Eucharist" means, "the giving of thanks." Mass is the most perfect way we can give gratitude to God for all the blessings we have received. That spirit of gratefulness should also overflow into our everyday lives as we will see in the final chapter.

Prayerfulness

After selecting the Twelve Apostles, Jesus sent them out to teach, to preach the Gospel or Good News, and to cure those who were sick. They later returned to Christ surely excited by the positive response to their teaching and by the many cures which their anointing with oil had produced. The Master, after hearing what they had done and taught, said to the Twelve: "Come away to a deserted place all by yourselves and rest a while." They were so surrounded by people coming and going that, not even having an opportunity to eat, the harried twelve "went away in the boat to a deserted place by themselves" (Mark 6:30–32).

As we have noted earlier, Jesus often retired to deserted places to pray, sometimes after strenuous periods of preaching and curing or, on other occasions, before making a major decision like the selection of the Twelve. All those who have walked in his footsteps since then have followed a similar pattern. They frequently and regularly stepped aside for quiet periods of prayerful reflection. These people knew that to carry a spirit of prayerfulness into their busy lives they needed moments of silent prayer away from the busyness.

The late great spiritual writer Father Henry Nouwen argued: "Those who do not set aside a certain place and time each day to do nothing but pray can never expect their unceasing thought to become unceasing prayers (*Clowning in Rome*, Garden City, New York: Image Books, 1979, pp. 61–62). The Church recognizes that

truth in its revised structure of the Mass. A prayerful attitude naturally should prevail throughout the liturgy; but to
facilitate this spirit, the regulations call for specific moments
of silence during the Eucharist. They mention, as examples,
reflective pauses after the invitation to pray in the beginning, following a reading or homily, and after Communion.

The entire Eucharist is meant to be our supreme
prayer. Setting aside a specific daily time for quite reflection outside of Mass and observing the desired pauses for
silence within Mass will help us maintain a spirit of prayerfulness throughout the entire eucharistic liturgy.

Cross Stamped

The Acts of the Apostles describes the life of the
early Church. In the second and fourth chapters it gives an
idyllic description of the first Christian communities (Acts
2:42–47; 4:32–35). Both sections reveal among those initial followers of Jesus a certain vertical, transcendent, or
sacred element. They devoted themselves to the breaking
of the bread in their homes and to the prayers; everyone
was filled with awe; they met together for prayer in the
temple; the apostles among them worked signs and wonders; they praised God; those first Christians with power
bore witness to the resurrection of the Lord Jesus; and all
enjoyed great favor or grace.

Both sections, however, also revealed a horizontal,
down-to-earth, community element. All those who
believed were together and shared everything in common,
sold their possessions and divided the results with others

according to their needs, ate meals with exultation and sincerity of heart, daily received new members into their midst, were of one mind and heart, and there was no needy person among them. We could say that they imaged a cross-stamped attitude in their lives and actions, a merging of the vertical, transcendent, and sacred with the horizontal, earthy, and communal.

The Mass, and those who participate in it, reflect or should reflect that same double or cross-stamped dimension. But there is certain tension involved when we merge those ingredients. Some years ago at a religious education conference in Pennsylvania the lay speaker mentioned how we formerly folded our hands at Mass. Now, he observed, we join hands as at the sign of peace. The man welcomes and enjoys this new (or restored) gesture of reconciliation, but wonders if we should not also retain the prior folding of hands. It is not a matter, in his judgment, of either/or, but of both/and.

That blend I would call cross-stamped. Integrating both is a delicate task. For example, during the course of every eucharistic liturgy we move from singing a song to listening in silence, from kneeling in awesome wonder before the Risen Lord to standing and reciting together the creed, from turning toward our neighbor with the sign of peace to reflecting in individual, private fashion for a few moments after receiving communion.

The presiding priest more than anyone else is the one who can best facilitate this delicate blending of the vertical and horizontal. But if the participants understand, welcome, and strive for that cross-stamped approach, his efforts at integration will be easier and more effective.

Joy

The forty hours which followed the burial of Christ into the tomb until his Easter resurrection were indeed dark moments for his followers. When Mary Magdalene and the other Mary came to inspect the tomb, there was suddenly an earthquake and an angel of the Lord who descended from heaven. The heavenly visitor rolled back the large stone before the tomb and sat upon it. His appearance seemed like a flash of lightning and his garments dazzled like snow. The guards, paralyzed at this sight, fell down like dead men. The angel then spoke to the frightened women, reassured them, invited them to look at the spot where Christ had been laid, told them that Jesus had been raised, and instructed the two quickly to inform the disciples about the resurrection and how the Master had gone ahead to Galilee where they would see him. The women hurried away, "fearful yet overjoyed" or, in another translation, "half-overjoyed, half-fearful." They ran, carrying the good news, the gospel, to Christ's disciples (Matt 28:1–8).

Joy happens when we are one with someone we love. That someone naturally could be a spouse, but the oneness may also be with family, relatives, friends, or God. Joy is not so much an attitude with which we receive our most welcome guest, Christ in the Eucharist. It is more a product of the presence, whether in the sacrifice of the

Mass, at Holy Communion, or before the Divine Lord reserved in the tabernacle.

I have seen in two retreat houses this same wonderful statement, but attributed to different persons: "Joy in the inevitable sign of the presence of God." As we have learned earlier, St. Thomas Aquinas would agree. Holy Communion, as food and drink, does delight us, brings us joy.

At weddings, I regularly urge the bride and groom to strive always for oneness. While perfect oneness comes only in the world to come, we all do experience, and those married couples especially, occasions of such unity. What happens when that occurs? Joys are doubled (birth of a child) and sorrows are cut in half (death of a parent). The Eucharist often gives us such a oneness in Christ. That unity with God automatically fills the heart with joy.

There is another inner quality which we need to address: an open heart. That will serve as the basis for the next and last chapter.

Catechism of the Catholic Church

> Those who receive the Eucharist are united
> more closely to Christ. Through it Christ
> unites them to all the faithful in one
> body—the Church. Communion renews,
> strengthens, and deepens this incorpora-
> tion into the Church, already achieved by
> Baptism. In Baptism we have been called
> to form but one body.* (No. 1396)

*Cf. 1 Cor 12:13.

CHAPTER SIX
Inspiration

*B*eing a Eucharistic Minister means to me: helping everyone. Many years ago I became a Eucharistic Minister to the housebound, helping the rector by visiting parishioners in their houses and bringing them the Holy Eucharist, for which they were very appreciative.

In Chapter 25 of St. Matthew's Gospel, Jesus speaks about how well or poorly we have led our lives and what to expect when eventually we go before God our judge. Christ does so through two parables—of the ten virgins and of the several talents—and then through the famous and often-quoted story of the shepherd, the sheep, and the goats.

The sheep will inherit the kingdom of eternal life prepared for them from the foundation of the world; the goats will go off to eternal punishment. Why the different destinations? The King (God, Jesus) posed this challenge: I was hungry, thirsty, a stranger, naked, ill, or in prison. The sheep responded to my various needs; the goats ignored them. Whatever they did or did not do to one of these least ones, they did or did not do to me.

This sheep and goats teaching should leave us all uncomfortable. Who perfectly lives out that injunction: Whatever you do to the least of my brothers or sisters you do to me? Jesus calls us to develop open hearts. If we believe that everything comes from God on high, that everything is a gift, then being grateful and expressing our gratitude flows naturally from that faith. God, however, also reminds us that we should be willing to share a portion of these gifts with others, thus making this a better world and building up the church.

Official Inspiration

The Mass's formal structure and directives for its celebration encourage this open-hearted spirit.

- The *General Intercessions* or *Prayer of the Faithful* leads the people gathered for worship to speak out on behalf of the church; the world; civil authorities; those oppressed by any burden; and the local community; especially those who are sick or have died.

- Church regulations for Mass encourage money or other gifts for the poor or for the Church to be brought forward with the bread, water, and wine, and placed in the sanctuary near the altar.
- At the end of Mass, the priest or deacon sends each member of the congregation to do good works, praising and blessing the Lord. That dismissal follows one of three options: "Go in the peace of Christ"; "The Mass is ended, go in peace"; or "Go in peace to love and serve the Lord."

Having been nourished by the Holy Spirit in the Liturgy of the Word and by Christ's Body and Blood in the Liturgy of the Eucharist, we go forth to make this a better world and build up the Church.

Helpful Texts

The Church's official books for Mass, the sacramentary and lectionary, provide rich and helpful texts for various celebrations connected with current needs.

• Many parishes have found that Thanksgiving Day Masses, with some creative effort, attract great crowds and deeply touch people. Appropriate music and readings; a reflective homily giving participants a silent opportunity to identify blessings received over the past year; a procession during which each individual brings an item of the food for the poor; loaves of bread, baked and blessed for the feast and distributed at the end of Mass, one per household—these ingredients make the Thanksgiving Day Eucharist a well-received event. In addition, Mass texts approved for the United States, like this Opening Prayer, speak to that holiday's theme:

> Father all powerful,
> your gifts of love are countless
> and your goodness infinite.
> On Thanksgiving Day we come before you
> with gratitude for your kindness:
> open our hearts to concern for our
> fellow men and women,
> so that we may share your gifts in
> loving service.

• Similarly, texts for Independence Day celebrations echo the open-hearted spirit, like this Prayer after Communion:

> God our Father
> through the food we have received
> you bless and sanctify us and the
> fruit of our toil.
> Help us to serve each other in justice
> and mercy and share what we have
> for the welfare of all men and women.

• When special circumstances arise, the ritual books contain a wealth of pertinent texts. After 9/11, Americans were seeking a spiritual response to this terrible event. On the Day of Prayer, as directed by the President, an overflow of two thousand people at our Cathedral looked for guidance and strength. The Opening Prayer for a Mass "In Time of War or Civil Disaster" perfectly fit the situation:

> God of power and mercy,
> You destroy war and put down earthy pride.
> Banish violence from our midst
> and wipe away our tears
> that we may all deserve to be called
> your son and daughter.

Direct Charity and Social Justice

Our open-hearted responses to the needs of others fall into two categories: direct deeds of charity or social justice actions. Feeding the hungry, visiting the imprisoned, and clothing the naked would be examples of direct charity. These tend to be individualized, hands-on, temporary solutions to poverty. Changing structures, advocating for those in need, and eliminating the causes of poverty are illustrations of social justice. These tend to be more community oriented, somewhat elusive or controversial, and geared to long-term resolutions of poverty conditions.

In the following three pastoral illustrations, you may find it instructive to categorize the various activities according to direct charity or social justice efforts.

Assisi in Syracuse

Assisi in *Syracuse* is a creative, diversified Franciscan Community endeavor to reach out to those in need throughout the city. They serve twelve thousand people monthly with soup and a sandwich or their equivalent, respond to many households with baskets from their food pantry, offer a health clinic staffed by volunteer medical personnel, make free legal advice available through the donated services of a half-dozen local attorneys, offer a residence for Sudanese refugees, and open their space for neighborhood meetings.

Our Own Cathedral

Our own *Cathedral* operates a Cathedral Emergency Services center, which caters to four hundred to five hundred households a month, regardless of background, from its food pantry and with advocacy guidance from caseworkers, hosts a hot breakfast program for 75–100 homeless men every Wednesday morning, and, at great expense, supports a kindergarten through grade six inner city Catholic school, the majority of whose students are African-American and from below poverty-level homes.

Seven years ago the parish initiated a Guardian Angel Society designed to raise funds from alumni, parishioners, and friends for the school and its students. Monies realized were to be used for helping those in need to attend the school, enhancing its technology and assisting with scholarships graduates of the Cathedral to attend

Catholic junior and senior high schools. The effort has enjoyed remarkable success, both in raising $1.1 million and in having a very positive impact upon the young boys and girls.

A dozen years ago many of the school's graduates never finished high school. Family obstacles and a negative surrounding culture led them to drop out. From the Guardian Angel Society's beginning, it has provided partial scholarships for those graduates wishing to go on to Catholic institutions and secured matching amounts from the schools themselves, which allowed the parents to pay the affordable tuition difference.

This year the Society contributed $16,000 to 26 students now in Junior and Senior high schools. Moreover, four of its graduates, completing six years of secondary education with Guardian Angel help, will enter college in the fall. Two of them have been accepted and given sizeable scholarships at Notre Dame and Georgetown. The Society contributed a modest amount to each of them, covering the necessary initial deposit.

Holy Cross Church

Holy Cross Church in *Vero Beach* on Florida's east coast, cited earlier in a different context, is a large parish, many congregants of which are fairly affluent retirees. The following list of efforts for the area's needy indicates how open are their hearts:

- Once a month parishioners bring packages of food to Mass. After the final liturgy, they need two pickup trucks for transporting the accumulated massive amount to a local soup kitchen.

- On a January weekend, 42 teenagers and 30 adults painted and repaired homes and cleaned up yards for the elderly and handicapped in Indian River County. On that same date, three teenage parishioners joined other students from the local Catholic high school to repair two homes and paint a Salvation Army distribution center.

- A regular collection on behalf of Habitat for Humanity will eventually reach $35,000, enough to sponsor another home. Over the past decade they have indirectly built fifty of these homes.

- The parish recently donated to the local Samaritan Center $58,039, which included a gift of stock.

- Two cars in the parking lot, an SUV and Cadillac sedan, had open windows and hand printed signs which read: "Blankets needed—throw inside cars." This is one family's personal project—supplying a homeless shelter with these blankets.

- Another family, working collaboratively with a local bicycle shop, takes repaired bikes to a migrant camp some miles inland from Vero Beach, where they are warmly welcomed by the workers there.

Active participation in the Eucharist clearly is the inspiration behind that impressive array of efforts for those in need.

The six weekend Masses at Holy Cross are crowded, some of them with standing room only. Four hundred to five hundred people worship at weekday Eucharists. A special chapel for adoration of the exposed Blessed Sacrament draws people for quiet prayer from early morning until late in the evening.

In that Florida parish the Eucharist obviously is the source and summit of its Christian life. There, the open hearts of its members flow from the Eucharistic Sacrifice, Sacrament, and Presence. Conversely, their many activities serving others lead back to the Eucharist, a mystery of our faith.

Catechism of the Catholic Church

St. John Chrysostom..."Not to enable the poor to share in our goods is to steal from them and deprive them of life. The goods we possess are not ours, but theirs."* (No. 2446)

---

*St. John Chrysostom, *Hom. in Lazaro* 2, 5: PG 48, 992.

Acknowledgments

I give thanks to several individuals for their invaluable help with this book about the Eucharist: Lawrence Boadt, CSP, publisher of Paulist Press, who with great persistence and much encouragement urged me to write the present volume and a previous one, *The Breaking of the Bread: An Updated Handbook for Extraordinary Ministers of Holy Communion*; Paul McMahon, Managing Editor at Paulist Press, for his hard work on both texts; Bishop Thomas J. Costello, for his typically thorough and positive review of my manuscripts; the extraordinary Ministers of Holy Communion at Syracuse Cathedral of the Immaculate Conception for their testimonies, which begin each chapter; and Ann Tyndall, who had to struggle with my difficult hand-written pages and turn them into a computerized manuscript.

Several books or articles were most useful as resource material:

"A Full Service Parish" (*Priest*, June 2004); *Behind Closed Doors* (Paulist Press); *Catechism of the Catholic Church* (United States Conference of Catholic Bishops); *General Instruction of the Roman Missal* (United States Conference of Catholic Bishops); *In the Presence of Our Lord* (Our Sunday Visitor); *Introduction to the Order of Mass* (United States Conference of Catholic Bishops); *Order for the Solemn Exposition of the Holy Eucharist* (Liturgical Press); *The Mystery and Meaning of the Mass* (Crossroads); *The Rites* (Pueblo); and *Summa Theologica of St. Thomas Aquinas* (Christian Classics).

Martin Hellriegel's mother, while pregnant with him, walked many miles to a German Shrine honoring the Precious Blood of Christ. She stayed two days, first asking for a healthy baby, and second, if the child was a boy, that he become a priest. Both wishes were granted.

Monsignor Hellriegel eventually served as a visionary pastor at Holy Cross Church in St. Louis and as a wise, informed, and remarkable leader in the liturgical movement during the middle of the last century. A telephone call asking about his condition would invariably elicit this response: "I am already looking forward to tomorrow's Mass which has been, is now, and I pray always will be the center of my life."

He lived for about ninety years, blind the last half-dozen of them. However, he had a eucharistic prayer memorized, invited someone to proclaim the assigned scripture readings at Mass, celebrated, and preached every day.

His faith in the Eucharist and love for the Mass should be inspiration to all of us.

Father Joseph M. Champlin
Cathedral of the Immaculate Conception
Syracuse, New York